THE BATTLE OF BRITAIN

Catherine Chambers

raintree
a Capstone company — publishers for children

Raintree is an imprint of Capstone Global Library Limited, a company incorporated in England and Wales having its registered office at 264 Banbury Road, Oxford, OX2 7DY – Registered company number: 6695582

www.raintree.co.uk
myorders@raintree.co.uk

Text © Capstone Global Library Limited 2017
The moral rights of the proprietor have been asserted.

Edited by Helen Cox Cannons
Designed by Steve Mead
Original illustrations © Capstone Global Library Limited 2017
Picture research by Ruth Smith
Production by Victoria Fitzgerald
Originated by Capstone Global Library Limited
Printed and bound in China

ISBN 978 1 4747 3421 9
20 19 18 17 16
10 9 8 7 6 5 4 3 2 1

British Library Cataloguing in Publication Data
A full catalogue record for this book is available from the British Library.

Acknowledgements
We would like to thank the following for permission to reproduce photographs: Alamy: Chronicle, 19, 20, Trinity Mirror/Mirrorpix, 16, War Archive, 11;Dreamstime: Andrew Oxley, 15; Getty Images: Evening Standard, 25, Fox Photos, 7; Glow Images: Heritage Images, 13; © IWM (CH 1429), 24; Newscom: Everett Collection, 8, KEYSTONE Pictures USA/ZUMAPRESS, 28, Mirrorpix, 17, 22, 26, MSI Mirrorpix, 10, News Syndication, 27, Not Known NI Syndication, 18; Shutterstock: Alfonso de Tomas, 29b, Amy Johansson, background design element, Andreas Berheide, cover, back cover, charnsitr, 29t, chrisdorney, 5t, 9, 14, Everett Historical, cover, back cover, 6, javarman, background design element, Ron Ellis, 23, Sergei A. Tkachenko, 15b, ShaunWilkinson, 15tl, Tomas Picka, cover, Willequet Manuel, background design element; Thinkstock: Matt_Gibson, 5.

We would like to thank Dr Stephen Bowman at the University of the Highlands and Islands for his invaluable help in the preparation of this book.

Every effort has been made to contact copyright holders of material reproduced in this book. Any omissions will be rectified in subsequent printings if notice is given to the publisher.

All the internet addresses (URLs) given in this book were valid at the time of going to press. However, due to the dynamic nature of the internet, some addresses may have changed, or sites may have changed or ceased to exist since publication. While the author and publisher regret any inconvenience this may cause readers, no responsibility for any such changes can be accepted by either the author or the publisher.

For my mother, Clare Bunter (1924–2016), a Land Army girl. CC

CONTENTS

BEFORE THE BATTLE

In 1940, during World War II, **Nazi** German forces attempted to attack Great Britain. They began by bombing the ports and Royal Navy bases of southern England. Between 10 July and 31 October that year, Britain's Royal Air Force (RAF) **Fighter Command** took to the skies to defend its shores. This period in the summer of 1940 is known as the Battle of Britain.

WHY DID GERMANY WANT WAR?

During World War I (1914–1918), Great Britain and its **Allies** defeated Germany and other countries. Germany was punished for its part in the war. As a result, many of its people starved. In 1933, Adolf Hitler became Chancellor of Germany. He promised the German people that Germany would be great once more under his new National Socialist Workers' Party, known as the Nazis.

POWER AND REVENGE

Adolf Hitler became popular during the 1930s by giving people work on public building projects, such as motorways (*autobahns*). He set up factories to build weapons, warships and fighter planes. Hitler had served as a soldier during World War I. He was angry about **territory** that Germany lost after the war. He urged Germans to support him and get this land back.

GREAT BRITAIN SLEEPS

Great Britain was also going through hard times. This period was called the **Depression**. The British government did not want to spend money on building lots of military weapons. So most of Britain's weapons and machinery became outdated. However, it did **invest** in aircraft development. This proved to be a good move.

CHURCHILL SAYS...

"Germany is arming – rapidly arming – and no one will stop her."

> By 1936, 63,000 men were trained as pilots or for technical support.

RISING TENSIONS

Once he was in power, Adolf Hitler became a dictator. This meant he gained total power over Germany and those who lived there. Between 1933 and 1938, the Nazis gradually gained control of Germany's neighbouring countries. In 1938, Hitler's government formed a union with Austria, called *Anschluss*. This meant that Austria was now ruled by Nazi Germany.

Hitler then wanted to take over a part of Czechoslovakia (now the Czech Republic and Slovakia) called the Sudetenland. He saw it as Germany's "natural territory". Surrounding countries and Great Britain wanted to avoid war at all costs. Hitler had stated that he would not **invade** the whole of Czechoslovakia if he could have the Sudetenland. Some leaders believed him. However, there were growing fears that Hitler could not be trusted. Britain began to gather its forces in case of war.

This photo of Adolf Hitler was taken in 1939. This was at the start of World War II.

"PEACE FOR OUR TIME"

Some British politicians, including Winston Churchill, were getting nervous. Churchill had been warning the government about the threat of Adolf Hitler for a long time. Britain's Prime Minister, Neville Chamberlain, still tried to keep the peace with Hitler. He met with him in Munich, Germany, on 15 September 1938 and agreed that Germany could take the Sudetenland. But other territories must be left alone.

Neville Chamberlain returned to London feeling triumphant. "I have returned from Germany with peace for our time," he declared proudly. However, agreements meant nothing to Hitler. Nazi forces marched into the Sudetenland on 1 October 1938. Then, in March 1939, Nazi troops and tanks took over the rest of Czechoslovakia. On 1 September 1939, Germany invaded Poland. Two days later, Great Britain and France declared war on Germany.

‹ Neville Chamberlain returned from meeting Hitler waving a peace agreement in his hand.

BLITZKRIEG - "LIGHTNING ATTACK"!

On 10 May 1940, two important events happened: German troops **invaded** Belgium, Holland and France in a surprise attack named *Blitzkrieg* ("Lightning attack"); and in Great Britain, Winston Churchill became Prime Minister.

Nazi troops marched into Belgium, Holland and France. Nazi Germany quickly took over those countries.

The British Expeditionary Force (BEF) and the 52nd Canadian Armoured Division fought hard to help the French Army in France. But the BEF was armed with old World War I rifles, machine guns and anti-tank guns. Germany, on the other hand, had well-armed troops and fast Panzer tanks. The German Air Force, named the *Luftwaffe*, helped the German army push back the BEF and its **Allies** to French seaports such as Dunkirk. Here, they were trapped.

CHURCHILL SAYS...

"... the Battle of France is over. I expect that the Battle of Britain is about to begin. Upon this battle ... depends our own British life ... and our Empire."

18 June, 1940

DEFEAT AND DEFIANCE

Between 26 May and 4 June 1940, Britain's Royal Navy and Royal Air Force came to the rescue by evacuating people from Dunkirk. They were joined by hundreds of ordinary, unarmed little fishing and pleasure boats. Together, they took Allied troops back to Britain, under heavy *Luftwaffe* fire. In all, 558 000 **Allied** servicemen, mostly British, Canadian, Australian and French, were saved. But many thousands were killed or taken prisoner.

By June 1940, the Nazis had control of mainland Europe. The thin, 33-kilometre (21-mile) strip of water named the English Channel was the only barrier between Great Britain and Nazi-held **territory**. On a clear day, anxious Britons standing at the Port of Dover could see France. From France, Nazi Germany was poised to attack by air and sea.

THE BATTLE BEGINS

On 10 July 1940, the *Luftwaffe* launched its first air attack on Great Britain. It aimed at Britain's shipping **convoys** and ports. The **Nazis** hoped this would crush the Royal Navy by 15 September. This was the date that they planned to begin Operation Sealion, a sea invasion of Britain.

A RAPID RESPONSE

Hitler's *Luftwaffe* bombers and fighter planes headed for Great Britain. In a deep, hidden **bunker** in Uxbridge, work in an Operations Room for southern England's **RAF** No. 11 Group was in full swing. Telephones were soon ringing. Volunteer aircraft spotters from the **Observer Corps** lined up along Britain's south coast.

This photograph, taken in 1940, shows Observer Corps at work, watching and reporting on all plane movements.

COORDINATE, PLOT...

In the bunker, Women's Auxilliary Air Force (WAAF) controllers listened to all the information crackling through their headphones. Observer Corps reported a swarm of far-off German aircraft. **Radar** screens confirmed it. Soon, WAAF plotters were mapping out approaching aircraft **formations** on a huge chart. Their wooden markers edged forward bit by bit as the *Luftwaffe* approached Great Britain's shoreline.

DECISION TIME

RAF senior officers hovered around the control table, watching closely. They must not send British pilots up to attack too soon. They would have to fly too far and their fuel would run out. Shot-down airmen would float out to sea and be beyond rescue. But if the *Luftwaffe* came too close, they could fly under the radar system.

Then the right moment had arrived. It was time to ...
"SCRAMBLE!"

WAAF plotters in action at Uxbridge in 1942.

A DAY IN THE LIFE OF A FIGHTER PILOT

4.30 a.m.

The hut is freezing. I'm shaken awake by the airman **orderly**. I pull on my trousers, fleece-lined leather jacket and boots.

4.40 a.m.

Ground crew check my *Spitfire*. I warm up the engine and check the equipment.

6.55 a.m.

We wait. "SCRAMBLE!" Ground crew is warming the engine. We pull on our parachutes, gloves and helmets. Twelve *Spitfires* take to the air. We get into **formation**.

7.05 a.m.

At 290 kilometres (180 miles) per hour we climb to 1,524 metres (5,000 feet). We reach our limit of 580 kilometres (360 miles) per hour and go straight into a dark cloud of **Luftwaffe**.

7.10 a.m.

A *Messerschmitt* fires at me. I bank to the left and dive. I climb again and fire back at it.

7.20 a.m.

We soar, break up, fire, dive, climb, get back in formation and fire again. In my headphones I can hear a babble of voices.

8.40 a.m.

I look down. Tilbury Docks are ablaze. German bombs have got through. My ammo (ammunition) is running out. I head for home.

8.45 a.m.

I land my *Spitfire*. The ground crew sprint up. They refuel, reload and repair the planes. The next **squadron** has already scrambled to face the *Luftwaffe*.

9.00 a.m.

I watch the other pilots in my squadron landing. Have we all made it? Yes. Now we go and eat.

9.15 a.m.

Some shiny new planes land – first a *Hurricane* then a *Spitfire*. Women Air Transport Auxilliary pilots bring new planes for new pilots when the old ones don't return.

10.45 a.m.

We are waiting for orders to take off again. Some people are chatting while others stare into space...

"SCRAMBLE!"

BATTLE FACTS

The average age of a fighter pilot was 20. The average pilot died aged just 22.

ACES AND AIRCRAFT

Most fighter pilots received training of just 3 hours on the ground and 30 hours in the air before starting. The ones who brought down the most enemy aircraft became heroes and were known as Aces. Aircraft designers and the factory workers who built the planes also helped to win the Battle of Britain.

A BATTLE OF NUMBERS

General Hermann Göring was head of the *Luftwaffe*. At the start of the Battle of Britain, he and Adolf Hitler believed that they faced 125 **RAF** fighter planes. However, Great Britain's Minister for Aviation, Lord Beaverbrook, had actually ordered over 400 planes each month during June, July and August. This poor **intelligence** helped defeat the *Luftwaffe*.

Another problem for the *Luftwaffe* was that there were never enough aircraft supplies. This forced exhausted *Luftwaffe* pilots to fight in up to seven sorties (trips) a day. RAF pilots fought no more than four.

CHURCHILL SAYS...

"Never in the field of human **conflict** was so much owed by so many to so few."

About Great Britain's fighter pilots, 20 August 1940

FIGHTER PLANES

BRITISH RAF FIGHTER PLANES

HURRICANE

Strengths – the first fighter to exceed 483 kilometres (300 miles) per hour. It could turn easily.

Weakness – its slow climbing speed stopped it from flying above trouble.

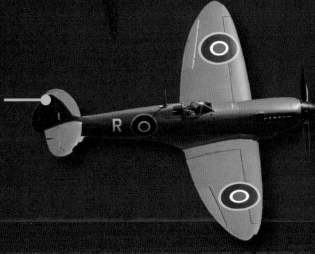

SPITFIRE

Strengths – light, very fast and could turn easily.

Weakness – it crumpled when hit.

GERMAN *LUFTWAFFE* FIGHTER PLANES

MESSERSCHMITT BF 109

Strengths – powerful, fast and could carry lots of weaponry.

Weakness – it could not fly far.

MESSERSCHMITT BF 110

Strengths – could travel long distances. It could dive and fire rapidly.

Weakness – it could not turn easily.

FACING THE BLITZ

Adolf Hitler's bombing campaign on British coastal ports failed. On 13 August 1940, the *Luftwaffe* launched an airborne assault named Operation Eagle Attack. This targeted air bases, aircraft factories and **radar**. Then, on 24 August, the *Luftwaffe* accidentally dropped bombs on south London streets instead of docks. The **RAF retaliated** by bombing Berlin, Germany's capital city. Great Britain waited to see how Germany would react.

Bristol was one of the cities to be badly hit by the bombing.

THE BLITZ

Nazi Germany's response was devastating. On 7 September, the skies over London filled with a dark swarm of enemy aircraft. From this time, London, Coventry, Plymouth, Bristol and many other cities were bombed to bits.

"WE CAN TAKE IT"

Adolf Hitler thought that the Blitz would break the British people's spirit. Instead, "We can take it" became their defiant slogan. Many people did not leave their cities but stayed to defend them.

Many rich city-dwellers moved out to the country or hid in the basements of large houses. London's poor were at first refused access to cellars of public buildings. London's Underground train stations were finally opened up but were not always safe. In January 1941, a bomb fell on Bank station. One hundred people were either killed or injured.

ROYAL SUPPORT

King George VI (far right) and Queen Elizabeth (left) stayed in London, even after three bomb blasts on Buckingham Palace. Queen Elizabeth said, "I am glad we have been bombed. It makes me feel I can look the East End in the face."

AT HOME WHEN THE SIRENS WAILED

Indoors, blackout curtains were drawn across every window. Street wardens checked them in case tiny chinks of light attracted the *Luftwaffe* bombers. Wardens were also looking out for traitors who might signal to the enemy.

RUN FOR COVER!

Until May 1941, most bombing raids happened at night. "Wailing Winnie" sirens warned people to hurry along dark streets to bomb shelters. At home, families grabbed their gas masks and ran into basements or hid under staircases. Some squeezed into Morrison shelters, which were steel-topped tables. Others packed into curved, **reinforced** garden huts called Anderson shelters.

⌃ As well as being tables, Morrison shelters were protected beds. This one had two levels. Sometimes, whole families would squeeze into one during **air raids**.

SWEETS IN THE SHELTER

During an air raid, families hiding in Anderson shelters took food and flasks of tea with them. Children were given barley-sugar sweets to suck. This stopped their ears popping from the noise of the bombs.

UNDER THE RUBBLE

Bomb blasts reduced thousands of homes, schools and work places to rubble during the Blitz. Water gushed from shattered pipes. Gas hissed from damaged supply lines and electricity fizzed from broken wires. This put fire fighters in great danger as they tackled roaring blazes. Yet they bravely continued to look for people buried under the rubble, dead or alive.

During the war and long after it, children used bombsites as playgrounds, though unexploded bombs were still a danger. Some are unearthed even today.

GAS MASK DRILL

Schoolchildren had to practise gas mask **drill** every day. This was in case bombs containing poisonous gas exploded.
The instructions were:
1. Remove mask from box.
2. Put mask on face.
3. Check mask is fitted correctly.
4. Breathe normally.

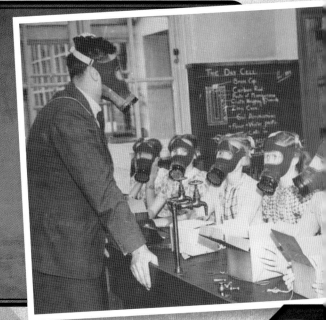

CHILDREN IN THE BLITZ

In September 1939, the British government prepared for bombs falling on London and other major cities. The government believed that children would be safer in the countryside. Over three days, around 1.5 million boys and girls, mothers with infants, and the elderly and infirm (weak) were sent away from cities. They were known as **evacuees**.

OPERATION PIED PIPER

The wartime evacuation was called Operation Pied Piper. In all, around 3 million evacuees left the cities. This included adults. Some evacuees sailed to Canada, South Africa, Australia and New Zealand.

Evacuees in south-east London wait for their train to arrive.

THE GREAT EVACUATION

Crowds of children gathered on railway platforms. Each child wore an identity label and carried a gas mask in its box. Adults unknown to the children supervised them. When they arrived, the children were taken to village halls. There, local people picked out the children they wanted. Some children enjoyed the countryside and were well cared for. Others were not.

WAS IT SAFER IN THE COUNTRYSIDE?

Kent is a large English county between the English Channel and London. Children were sent to Kent for safety. However Kent became known as "Bomb Alley". Here, many bombs fell. Some were strays or were dumped by *Luftwaffe* pilots when their fuel was low. A lighter load on their planes gave them a better chance of returning to their base across the Channel. Most of the British countryside, however, was safer and quieter.

TRANSFORMING THE COUNTRYSIDE

By June 1939, the British government was worried that **Nazi** Germany might try to starve Britain. It could do this by attacking ships carrying food from other countries. So the British government encouraged its farmers to produce more food for the nation. The British people even dug up their gardens to grow vegetables.

Some Land Girls, working on the harvest in 1940.

PLOUGH IT ALL UP!

Every scrap of farmland was ploughed up to grow crops. Wildflower meadows became wheat fields. With young men away at war, farmers needed help. The government recruited a Land Army of young women, as they had already done during World War I. The "Land Girls" worked in the fields, drove tractors or looked after livestock. They worked hard from dawn to dusk in summer and through dark, bitterly cold winters.

UNDER THREATENING SKIES

The *Luftwaffe* even threatened people in the countryside, as this story shows.

"I served in the Land Army. We cycled to the fields and sometimes bombers flew over while I was on my bike. We were told to jump into the nearest ditch. But I kept going and shook my fist up at them. Sometimes my friends and I were shot at by aircraft machine-guns. The government ordered us to keep this quiet. I suppose it was to stop people panicking. But it was true."

Clare Bunter, Chelmsford, Essex

HOW DO WE KNOW?

Many people wrote diaries during World War II. They wrote letters from home to their loved ones in the battlefields. In recent years, their stories have been recorded and are held in national libraries and museums.

The National Archives

< The National Archives building in London contains a large number of wartime documents.

A TURNING POINT IN THE WAR

In the early hours of 15 September 1940, southern England faced its toughest challenge yet. The *Luftwaffe* flew towards the Kent coast. They had 200 bombers and their fighter-plane **escorts**. The **Nazis** believed that the **RAF** had fewer aircraft left than they actually did.

A BATTLE PLAN

There were in fact 660 RAF aircraft at the ready. Air Command sent up 276 *Spitfires* and *Hurricanes* to meet the *Luftwaffe*. They had support on the ground from anti-aircraft guns. They followed a unique plan. It was called the Big Wing **strategy**.

The Big Wing strategy involved five RAF **squadrons** flying in an arrow-shaped wing **formation** towards the *Luftwaffe*. The formation allowed the squadrons on the side to pick up aircraft that shot through the front squadrons. This helped the RAF win the day.

The new wing formation was designed to look menacing.

BADER

In 1931, Douglas Bader lost a leg in a flying accident but still became the fifth most successful RAF fighter pilot during World War II. Bader created the Big Wing strategy with his commanding officer, Trafford Leigh-Mallory. Bader was shot down in France and imprisoned on 9 August 1941.

DEFEAT FOR THE *LUFTWAFFE*

By the end of that day, the RAF had shot down 185 German aircraft. The *Luftwaffe* planes flew back over the English Channel to Germany.

Luftwaffe pilots were exhausted and felt defeated.

German *Luftwaffe* pilot Roderich Cescotti remembers…

"We were shaken by the number of fighters the Royal Air Force was able to put up on the day … It was becoming clear that we were likely to break before the enemy."

BATTLE FACTS

Out of a total of 2,936 RAF Battle of Britain pilots, 574 were non-British volunteers. They came from Australia, Canada, the Caribbean islands, Czechoslovakia, France, Poland, South Africa and the United States.

BEYOND THE BATTLE

Great Britain's victory in the Battle of Britain denied the *Luftwaffe* a clear path to destroy its air force. This meant that Adolf Hitler had to **postpone** Operation Sealion – the invasion of Britain by sea.

Adolf Hitler brushed aside **Nazi** Germany's failure to defeat Great Britain. On 22 June 1941, Hitler instead turned his Nazi troops eastward to the **Soviet Union**. Here, his troops and tanks ended up stuck in a terrible **conflict** in a freezing snowbound winter.

Radar operators, such as this one, played a large part in Brtain's success against the *Luftwaffe*.

LESSONS LEARNED

On paper, the *Luftwaffe* had a clear advantage. They began the battle with more bombers and the same number of fighter planes as the British. But the *Luftwaffe* did not have a **consistent** plan of action. Also, Great Britain's **radar**, plotters, spotters and radio links had always made its War Office one step ahead of the Nazis.

A crowd in Whitehall, London, celebrate VE day.

JUST THE BEGINNING

RAF fighter pilots went on to support **Allied** invasions of North Africa, Sicily, Italy and southern France. Then, on 6 June 1944, came D-Day. Allied forces, which from December 1941 included the United States, joined together to storm northern France. D-day was the beginning of the end of World War II. The war in Europe finally ended with victory over Nazi Germany on 8 May 1945 (known as VE Day).

BATTLE FACTS

By 31 October 1940, the RAF had lost 1,495 airmen. Of these, 449 were fighter pilots, 718 were from Bomber Command and 280 were from Coastal Command.

BIOGRAPHY: WINSTON CHURCHILL

Winston Leonard Spencer-Churchill was born on 30 November 1874 at Blenheim Palace in Oxfordshire. He went to Harrow, a top school, then Sandhurst Military College. From there he became an officer in the British Army.

Churchill first worked as a **journalist** and travelled the world. Then, in 1900, he turned to politics and became a **Member of Parliament** (MP) for the town of Oldham in Lancashire. In 1911, Churchill became First Lord of the Admiralty. This meant he was in charge of the Royal Navy.

In 1940, during World War II, Churchill became Prime Minister. He was mostly a good leader and gave **inspirational** speeches. They helped the British people during difficult times. When World War II ended in 1945, Churchill said, "In all our long history, we have never seen a greater day than this."

Churchill died on the 24 January 1965, aged 90. Thousands of people lined the streets. Between 850 and 900 million people around the world watched his funeral on television.

TIMELINE

1940

JULY

10 JULY The Battle of Britain begins.

JULY The *Luftwaffe* bombs Great Britain's ports and Royal Navy bases.

16 JULY Adolf Hitler's navy is anchored off the coast of France. It is preparing for Operation Sealion – the invasion of Great Britain.

AUGUST

12 AUGUST **Nazi** Germany's **intelligence** realizes that **radar** is alerting Great Britain to its **air raids**. The *Luftwaffe* then decides to target radar stations.

13 AUGUST The *Luftwaffe* launches Operation Eagle Attack, attacking **RAF** bases, aircraft factories and radar. Bad weather stops total destruction.

15 AUGUST The *Luftwaffe* suffers heavy losses as German and British fighter planes go head to head. It becomes known as "Black Thursday" by Nazi Germany.

24 AUGUST *Luftwaffe* bombers accidentally drop bombs on south London streets instead of docks.

25 AUGUST The RAF **retaliates**, bombing Berlin.

SEPTEMBER

7 SEPTEMBER The Blitz begins. The *Luftwaffe* bombards London.

15 SEPTEMBER Battle of Britain Day. **Fighter Command** shoots down 56 *Luftwaffe* aircraft. Adolf Hitler realizes that daytime air raids are too risky and reduces them.

17 SEPTEMBER Adolf Hitler **postpones** Operation Sealion. Bombing continues.

OCTOBER

12 OCTOBER Operation Sealion is cancelled.

31 OCTOBER The last daylight raid takes place. The Battle of Britain is over.

GLOSSARY

air raid attack in which bombs are dropped to the ground by an aircraft

bunker underground shelter used during wartime

conflict battle

consistent staying the same all of the time

convoy group of aeroplanes or vehicles travelling together

Depression period of financial and industrial difficulties in a country. Great Britain experienced a major Depression between 1929 and 1932.

drill repeated training in something that may be needed in an emergency

escort person, vehicle or group accompanying another for protection

Fighter Command one of the special units of the RAF that ran the fighter planes during World War II

formation group of things organized in a certain pattern or arrangement

inspirational uplifting the mind and spirit

intelligence gathering of military or political knowledge

invade entering a country with an army and aiming to take it over

journalist person who writes for newspapers and magazines

Luftwaffe German air force

Member of Parliament (MP) someone who represents his or her local area in the House of Commons

Nazi member of the National Socialist German Workers' Party, the political party that ruled Germany during World War II

Observer Corps civil defence organization operating in Great Britain between 1925 and 1995. During the War, it was mostly made up of volunteers.

orderly soldier in charge of passing on instructions or orders

postpone put something off for a later time or date

radar device for locating moving objects and craft using radio signals

reinforced strengthened using additional material

retaliate fight back in response to an attack

Soviet Union empire in which Russia controlled neighbouring countries from 1917 to 1991. Its full name was the Union of Soviet Socialist Republics.

Spitfire single-seat, single-engined British fighter aircraft of World War II

squadron operational unit in an air force consisting of two or more flights of aircraft and their pilots

strategy plan of action designed to achieve a long-term or overall aim

territory area of land that is owned by a country or empire

FIND OUT MORE

BOOKS

Evacuation (Stories of World War II), A. J. Stone (Wayland, 2015)

Evacuation in World War II (The History Detective Investigates), Martin Parsons (Wayland, 2015)

Who Was Winston Churchill? Ellen Labrecque (Turtleback Books, 2015)

WEBSITES

http://primaryfacts.com/1247/the-battle-of-britain-facts-and-information/
This website gives interesting facts and information about the Battle of Britain.

http://www.primaryhomeworkhelp.co.uk/war/blitz.htm
Find out what life was like during the Blitz by reading this fascinating website.

PLACES TO VISIT

Imperial War Museum, Duxford, Cambridgeshire, CB22 4QR
http://www.iwm.org.uk/exhibitions/iwm-duxford/battle-of-britain
The Imperial War Museum at Duxford contains first-hand accounts and artefacts from World War II, including a real *Messerschmitt Bf 109*.

INDEX